THE LAND OF MANY COLORS

Written by
the Klamath County YMCA Family Preschool
Klamath Falls, Oregon

Illustrated by Rita Pocock

SCHOLASTIC INC.
NEW YORK TORONTO LONDON AUCKLAND SYDNEY

Library of Congress Cataloging-in-Publication Data

The land of many colors / written by the Klamath County YMCA Family
    Preschool. Klamath Falls, Oregon ; illustrated by Rita Pocock.
                    p. cm. — (My first library)
            Summary: Preschoolers present their views on resolving conflicts and
    solving problems.
            ISBN 0-590-49248-9
            1. Social conflict—Juvenile literature. 2. Conflict management—Juvenile
    literature. 3. Problem solving—Juvenile literature.
    [1. Conflict management. 2. Problem solving. 3. Interpersonal relations.
    4. Children's writings.] I. Pocock, Rita. ill. II. Klamath County YMCA Family
    Preschool. III. Series.
    HM136L37 1993
    303.6—dc20   92-31188
                                        CIP
                                        AC

Copyright © 1993 by Scholastic Inc.
Illustrations copyright © 1993 by Rita Pocock
Designed by Bill Smith Studio, Inc.
All rights reserved. Published by Scholastic Inc.
My First Library is a registered trademark of Scholastic Inc.
12 11 10 9 8 7 6 5 4 3 2 1   3 4 5 6 7 8/9
Printed in the U.S.A.
First Scholastic Printing, 1993

*To Diana Wiseman for
supporting us in all we do. – C.R.*

For Tekla – R.P.

These are the purple people.

They like purple food.
They have purple pets.
They think purple is best.

These are the blue people.
They like blue food.
They have blue pets.

They think blue is best.

These are the green people.

Can you guess what kind of
food they like?
What kind of pets do they have?

One day the purple people said,
"We need more toys."

The blue people said,
"We need more blue food."

And the green people said,
"We don't need anything
because we are the best."

Before they knew how it happened, they were all fighting and hurting each other!

It was **WAR!**

The houses were ruined.

The animals were hurt.

The plants were smashed.

All of their toys were broken.

The food was running out and everyone was sad.

Then one little child all covered
with dust walked up and said,

"ST

OP!

"Why are we hurting each other?
We are different, but we are the same."
Everyone looked at the little child.
Was he purple? Was he blue? Was he green?
No one could tell. He was just dusty.

"This war is mean," he said.
"It is scary. We should all be friends.
  We all have feelings that make us happy or sad.
  We all love animals and flowers and rainbows.
  We should learn to live together."

The different people looked
at each other. They smiled.
"He is right!" they shouted.

The war was over.

Soon they began to help
each other build houses.

Everyone helped to take care
of the animals.

They traded seeds among
one another for planting.
The people were happier.

There was still the problem of food.
There would only be enough food if
they mixed it all up and everyone
ate all of the different colors.
So they did.

They ate it. They loved it.
"This is better than anything," they shouted.
They were happy to all be friends.

**The Land of Many Colors became
a peaceful, loving world.**

Written by:

Kevin Bicknell
Lita Coriz
Travis Daily
Sam Dobresk
Justin Franks
Jason George
Sarah Gnadt
Maria Graybeal
Mandie Harris
Annie Harworth
Rachel Hawkins
Amanda Herron
Devon Hitson
Andrew Jones
Bradley Kiser
Matthew Lawler

Brandon Love
Samantha Pence
Tessa Rodgers
Julie Rosario
Kourtney Rusow
Tamera Shaw
Ali Shelley
Brian Smith
Justin Smith
Stephanie Sullivan
Margot (Mugsie) Thompson
Kirsten Tucker
Danielle Walker
Shane Walker
Jessica Westwood

Sande Jipp, assistant teacher
Charlotte Reyes, teacher/director

About This Book . . .

When I first read about the Scholastic *We Are Different ... We Are Alike* program, I saw a perfect way to combine our love of books with our feelings about the similarities and differences among people in the world.

As part of our curriculum we learn about and explore the similarities and differences of people in our community and around the world. This is always a favorite time of the year, as the children learn about their heritage and bring in things to share from all over the world. Songs in various languages, simple folk dances, and different instruments are explored. Part of this exploration includes an international potluck, where each family brings its favorite ethnic dish.

During the Persian Gulf War, the children had many questions about war since some had friends and family members involved. We incorporated our newly acquired knowledge of world differences and similarities to help understand what was happening. Our book, *The Land of Many Colors*, came out of our discussion and shared concerns about world peace.

We began by exploring the various parts of a book. Next, we decided what our book would be about. Each day I asked pertinent questions such as "What kind of people should we have? What are they like? What should happen in our story?" I kept notes on what the children were saying. Once we had our ideas down, it didn't take much to arrange them into a story written by us all. For our own special book each child created an illustration depicting a part of the story. For publication a professional illustrator has given our story a finished look that we all love.

The children have taken great pride in creating such a wonderful story to share with the world. Let's hope that many people hear what these children have to say.

Charlotte (Coco) Reyes
Preschool Teacher/Director
Klamath County YMCA Family Preschool
Klamath Falls, Oregon